LIVING GRATITUDE

28 DAYS OF PRAYER AND THANKSGIVING

Abingdon Press | Nashville

Living Gratitude:
28 Days of Prayer and Thanksgiving

Library of Congress Control Number: 2022930730

ISBN 978-1-7910-2406-2

22 23 24 25 26 27 28 29 30 31 — 10 9 8 7 6 5 4 3 2 1
MANUFACTURED IN THE UNITED STATES OF AMERICA

CONTENTS

There is power in gratitude. When we live in gratitude, we gain the strength to see God's grace everywhere. Anxiety loses its grasp on us, fear flees from our hearts, and we walk in the fullness of our calling. Jesus gave thanks with only five loaves of bread and two fish, and the abundance of Jesus's gratitude even in this scarcity was enough to feed all five thousand and more (Mark 6:30-44). Paul and Silas gave thanks to God when they were going through some serious mistreatment and persecution. Their audacity to live in gratitude opened the door for the precious opportunity to save a life, literally, as they prevented the prison jailer from harming himself. This birthed a cascade of impacts in the life of the jailer and he "believe[d] in the Lord Jesus" (Acts 16:16-40). Gratitude has such a power; it turns the scarcity mindset to one of abundance, and it transforms a limiting circumstance to an exciting opportunity.

With the rise of the pandemic in recent years, many of our churches perhaps struggle with the scarcity mindset. Many of us may be challenged by the new limitations and boundaries we call "the new normal." Some of us may be looking at the five loaves of bread and two fish in our hands, wondering how we can serve our mission fields as we are called to serve five thousand and more. We are in the midst of coping with many losses in our lives, and the divisions among us put so much more weight on our shoulders.

The church of Thessalonica was also going through a time of loss in the midst of challenges. With religious disagreements and political turmoil in their communities,

they were coping with the pain of losing their leaders, their social status, and their beloved ones. But the apostle Paul exhorted them even in these dire circumstances, "Rejoice always, pray without ceasing, give thanks in all circumstances; for this is the will of God in Christ Jesus for you" (1 Thessalonians 5:16-18). When Paul himself was again in a prison and the church of Philippi was in the middle of a serious division, he again exhorted them, "Do not be anxious about anything, but in every situation, by prayer and petition, with thanksgiving, present your requests to God" (Philippians 4:6 NIV). When we choose to give thanks instead of being anxious, we find God's peace that surpasses all understanding guarding our hearts and our minds in Christ Jesus (Philippians 4:7)! We see that gratitude is an essential part of our journey with God, especially when we find ourselves in difficult challenges.

Then, perhaps this is a prime time for us to offer the living sacrifice of thanksgiving and wholeheartedly live in gratitude. Our foremothers and forefathers of faith stood firm not through weapons, nor through abundance, but through simply giving thanks and walking in gratitude. The reason that they were "afflicted in every way, but not crushed; perplexed, but not driven to despair; . . . struck down, but not destroyed" is because they recognized the treasure in Christ Jesus and walked their lives in gratitude (2 Corinthians 4:7-10).

What is the treasure you find in Christ Jesus? What treasures can you find in your life and within you that you are called to faithfully steward and give thanks for? In such a time as this, perhaps one of the most powerful and prophetic ministries we can offer is to audaciously live in gratitude. So, we invite you to begin a journey of renewing this powerful spiritual practice of gratitude. For the next twenty-eight days, the diverse group of pastors, business and church leaders, speakers, and authors who have contributed to this book will walk alongside you as you begin this journey of gratitude. Each week has a focus theme: gratitude, generosity, prayer, and call. Gratitude leads us to generosity. Gratitude is an essential part of prayers, which empower us to walk in the fullness of God's calling in our lives.

We pray that at the end of this twenty-eight-day journey of gratitude, we experience God's grace that transforms our scarcity mindset to one of abundance and generosity. We pray that we find the power of the five loaves of bread and two fish in our hands through this sacred practice of gratitude. We pray that God gives each one of us wisdom to see our limiting and challenging circumstances as unique opportunities for working in the kingdom of God. In such a time as this, we pray that our practice of gratitude collectively will be a powerful prophetic voice to the world that speaks of God's goodness and love for all of us in the midst of these difficult challenges we face in our world.

So, friends, let us remember God's grace and be thankful. We look forward to your powerful witness of gratitude in such a time as this.

Rev. Danielle Buwon Kim

Then he said to him, "Get up and go on your way; your faith has made you well."

Luke 17:19

When the turn of the century saw an explosion of research into the beneficial effects of gratitude, I jumped right on board, filling notebooks with lists of people, circumstances, and things that made my life better. It seemed that science was confirming the old "count your blessings" adage with evidence of increased productivity and measurable satisfaction, and after a long span of personal dissatisfaction, I had plenty of blessings that needed counting. Each time I catalogued items I was thankful for, I walked away with renewed energy and optimism. But each time I stumbled over a new obstacle, that optimism crumbled. Between lists, I was only one flat tire, one broken sump pump, or one toddler meltdown away from ingratitude.

In the midst of my uncertainty, I came across Luke's account of Jesus and the ten lepers who roam the borderland between Samaria and Galilee, displaced from homes and families by levitical law. Although they come from inimical cultures, they cry out to Jesus in uniform despair, and when Jesus responds by sending them to the priest for inspection, the men find themselves restored along the way. When healing dissolves the suffering that had united them, the nine men who continue toward the

GRATITUDE

priest for ceremonial reintegration into their communities don't seem to miss the Samaritan man who hurries back to Jesus. My heart went out to those nine men who finished their journey to the priest. After all, they were obeying the command of the Healer! The Samaritan who returned had abandoned obedience to follow his own impulses, hadn't he? On the other hand, maybe he recognized the Healer as the true priest, and his cries of gratitude, which Jesus calls "praise," reflect wholehearted faith in a God who outlasts every temple. Falling at the feet of Jesus, the restored Samaritan is commended for his faith.

When I finished the story and looked back through my gratitude lists, I noticed that the only thread connecting my blessings was their net effect on me. I had become skilled at identifying things that I was thankful for, but I had entirely neglected to direct my gratitude toward the One I was thankful to. Like the nine lepers, I inhabited my healing with no further regard for the Healer. That afternoon marked a spiritual shift. Instead of propping up my tenuous contentment with lists of things that made me happy, I slowly began to thank God, directly, for creating and sustaining me, for designing and loving my family, for diffusing pink light into an inimitable sunrise, and for inventing the possibility of song. I gave thanks at the feet of the Priest who still ushers us into holy places even as we wander in the wilderness between temples. When I offer thanks to God in the sacred space of conversational prayer, gratitude becomes an act of worship, a declaration of faith in a God who remains constant, even when the good things around me give way.

Amy Linnemann

DAY TWO

Consider it pure joy, my brothers and sisters, whenever you face trials of many kinds, because you know that the testing of your faith produces perseverance. Let perseverance finish its work so that you may be mature and complete, not lacking anything.

James 1:2-4 NIV

When I was a kid, my family, like many others, would go around the dinner table at Thanksgiving and have everyone share one thing for which they were thankful. We would often say things like our home, our family, and the fun vacation we had that summer.

Once or twice, someone would mention something negative that happened, like being thankful for their doctor who got them through the big surgery they had that year. I never heard anyone say, "I'm thankful I got laid off from my job," or "I'm thankful for my divorce," or "I'm so thankful I have cancer."

Such statements would have brought an uncomfortable silence to the dinner table. How do you ask someone to pass the peas after they've disclosed a major life event like that?

In my years as a pastor, I've had the opportunity to walk with people through many difficult situations in life, and I've been surprised and inspired by the way some of them have responded to devastating news.

One man was diagnosed with inoperable cancer, and in the months he had left he took great pains to try to reconcile with friends and family members whose relationships had been strained. At his funeral, one of those relatives said if he had died in a car crash, they would live the rest of their life with regret over not forgiving each other.

"I feel weird saying this," his relative shared, "but I'm actually thankful that he got cancer, because probably nothing else would have led us to patch things up, and now we are both at peace."

Trials are a part of life, and there is nothing inherently good about the pain they cause. God does not put trials into our lives for the purpose of teaching us a lesson. Pain and struggle are part of the reality of living in a broken world. The writer of James invites us to broaden our perspective, because trials can give us the opportunity to grow.

On his children's TV show, *Mister Rogers' Neighborhood*, Fred Rogers told his audience that his mother told him when he got scared by things going on in the world to "look for the helpers." We experience God's grace in the people and things that help us get through tough times.

God does not cause people to get cancer. God walks with us through it and helps us make the best of the time we have left.

God does not cause people to get divorced or lose their jobs. God cries with us in our pain, sits with us in our grief, and helps us ask deep questions of ourselves so our brokenness can be part of our transformation to being more whole than we were before. God is present with us in the "in-between" spaces to nudge us toward new possibilities.

Maybe no one is going to specifically raise a glass to a pandemic or other trials this year, but we might be able to share our gratitude for how God walked with us through this time of trial.

Matthew L. Kelley

DAY THREE

*When you have eaten your fill and have built fine houses and live
in them, and when your herds and flocks have multiplied, and your silver
and gold is multiplied, and all that you have is multiplied, then do not exalt
yourself, forgetting the LORD your God, who brought you out of the land of
Egypt, out of the house of slavery, who led you through the great and terrible
wilderness, an arid wasteland with poisonous snakes and scorpions. He
made water flow for you from flint rock, and fed you in the wilderness with
manna that your ancestors did not know, to humble you and to test you, and
in the end to do you good. Do not say to yourself, "My power and the might
of my own hand have gotten me this wealth." But remember the LORD your
God, for it is he who gives you the power to get wealth.*

Deuteronomy 8:12-18

At a stop during the 2012 presidential campaign, Barack
Obama said, "If you've been successful, you didn't get there on your
own.... I'm always struck by people who think, well, it must be
because I was just so smart.... It must be because I worked harder
than everyone else."

One line in his remarks—"If you've got a business, you didn't
build that"—became immediately controversial. The broader con-
text, the idea that we succeed together and our prosperity is built in
part on the work of others, was lost.

Whether or not it made for smart politics, Obama's statement
would have made a good sermon. In fact, it sounds strikingly like a
sermon preached by Moses three thousand years earlier—a sermon
that speaks to our own prosperous, materialistic society.

As the Israelites neared the end of their wilderness sojourn,
Moses admonished them with a warning. Once you begin to pros-
per in the Promised Land of milk and honey, he said, you will be

tempted to think that you achieved this wealth with your own hands. But you didn't build that on your own. God is the power behind your success.

Moses's words call us to give continual thanks for God's blessings. In the unforgiving wilderness, the people had been meant to learn their complete dependence on God for survival. But prosperity can make us complacent over time. Moses knew that the people would eventually forget that God made possible everything they had and would come to take their blessings for granted.

Yet Moses's sermon also goes well beyond the calls to give thanks that are common in the Psalms. It was a statement as important to the ideal organization of ancient Israel's society as the opening words of the Declaration of Independence, which speak of God-given equality and inalienable rights, are to American ideals.

If everything is a gift entrusted to us by God, then everything ultimately belongs to God, and God can ordain how those gifts are used. God's law instructed farmers to leave a portion of their crops unharvested, so the poor could glean. It's not ultimately your field; it's God's. God dictated that all debts must be forgiven every seven years, regardless of how much was still owed.

It's why the prophet Isaiah insisted that true worship involves not fasting but taking care of the poor and the oppressed. It's why John the Baptist told his listeners that, under the rules of God's kingdom, "Whoever has two coats must share with anyone who has none; and whoever has food must do likewise" (Luke 3:11).

Time and again, Scripture reminds us that giving thanks is only the beginning. As God told Abraham, we are blessed to be a blessing. When we remember that it all belongs to God and respond accordingly, then, as Moses preached, we, all of us, can do well in the land God has given us.

Randy Horick

DAY FOUR

We want you to know, brothers and sisters, about the grace of God that has been granted to the churches of Macedonia; for during a severe ordeal of affliction, their abundant joy and their extreme poverty have overflowed in a wealth of generosity on their part.
2 Corinthians 8:1-2

Generosity—real generosity—makes no sense! The words in this Scripture make no sense. Read them again, "for during a severe ordeal of affliction, their abundant joy and their extreme poverty have overflowed in a wealth of generosity." God has blessed me with the amazing privilege of seeing, living, and receiving this kind of generosity that "makes no sense." On the outer edges of Siberia, a young Russian orphan taught me the meaning of generosity. As we said goodbye, tears in our eyes, this child who had nothing took his one possession, a small silver ring and held it out to me. He wanted me to take the ring. I said with tears running down my face, "Nyet, nyet, nyet." Our interpreter came to me and said, "Scott, you must take the ring—he is so grateful that you came and are his friend." And there was the key, the lesson of a lifetime: "He is so grateful." Without gratitude, generosity makes no sense. With heartfelt gratitude, genuine and even radical generosity makes perfect sense.

Nearly a decade later in a small village in Malawi, God repeated the lesson. During famine and with AIDS sweeping through the country like wildfire, we visited a small, isolated village. In this village, mothers were forced to choose which child they would feed. The pastor died due to hunger and AIDS. And yet as we prepared to leave, the villagers in a parade with dancing and singing offered us a gift—food. In a village where children were starving, they gave the wealthy Americans the gift of food. Once again, I protested, and once again, I heard those words, "You must take the food, they are so very grateful you came." With heartfelt gratitude, genuine and even radical generosity makes perfect sense.

How have you experienced the connection between gratitude and generosity? As you consider your relationship to your church and God: what are you most deeply grateful for? Does your generosity match your gratitude?

Thank you, God, for the people who show us the true meaning of generosity. With all I have, help me be truly grateful and genuinely, radically generous.

Scott McKenzie

DAY FIVE

Some wandered in desert wastes,
finding no way to an inhabited town;
hungry and thirsty,
their soul fainted within them.
Then they cried to the LORD in their trouble,
and [the LORD] delivered them from their distress;
[the LORD] led them by a straight way,
until they reached an inhabited town.
Let them thank the LORD for [the LORD's] steadfast love,
for [the LORD's] wonderful works to humankind.
For [the LORD] satisfies the thirsty,
and the hungry [the LORD] fills with good things.
Psalm 107:4-9

The biblical narrative is rooted in an understanding of abundance: God is enough for humanity, God protects humanity, and a kingdom on earth as it is in heaven. However, even as we have been given a birthright of abundance, when we are facing scarcity, it can make us unable to trust what we cannot see.

Psalm 107 focuses on the interaction between humanity and the Lord. It is important to note that their interactions are fully in response to each other. A group of humans were wandering in a desert and not seeing a path to safety and health. Is that you right now, or can you think of a time when you were hopelessly lost and didn't know what needed to happen to find hope?

When humanity cried to the Lord in the midst of their turmoil, God delivered them. God did not erase their troubles or change their reality instantly—God instead led them into a new path where they had to take the first steps. They most likely did not know where they were going. This is important—they followed God's instructions without knowing what the outcome would be.

The people arrived in a town that was described as "inhabited"—not a land overflowing with wealth, food, and resources, but a town that had people. The biblical narrative of abundance sometimes refers to material goods and money, but more often the redemption of brokenness comes from relationships with others, and when we care for the stranger.

The Lord led the lost people into relationship, and they found what they needed. It may not have been what they were looking for, but it helped them have enough. And in response they showed gratitude to God.

God provides, and God's provision often comes in unexpected ways. As you are deepening your practice and understanding of stewardship, consider how God is pointing you in the direction of the unexpected, and give thanks that God is willing to surprise us all.

April Casperson

Rejoice always, pray without ceasing, give thanks in all circum-
stances; for this is the will of God in Christ Jesus for you.
1 Thessalonians 5:16-18

The months following my college graduation found me par-
alyzed by the prospect of discerning and following God's will for
my life. Untangling a calling from the intractable knot of passions
that marked my early twenties left me frustrated and confused.
While the church narrative I grew up with promised direction from
Scripture and the Holy Spirit, I wrestled with questions that led to
dead ends and wide-open spaces, without any signposts or clearly
marked paths for me to follow. In a fit of despair, I reached out to
my pastor father, expecting him to point me toward some chapter
and verse that would snap everything into focus. Instead, he met
my anguish with studied compassion. "You are worrying around
the edges of God's will like it's a tent, like if you step too far one
way or another, you'll be left out in the rain," he explained. "Jesus
offers freedom that's much more like an umbrella. Keep it open and
go where you want to! You're not going to end up somewhere that
God's will won't reach."

When I read today's passage from Paul's first letter to the people
of Thessalonica, I'm reminded of that umbrella. "Rejoice always,
pray continually, give thanks in all circumstances; for this is God's
will for you in Christ Jesus" (NIV). God's will, as Paul described it,
is not tied to a career or a calling but a way of living. Joy, prayer,
and gratitude characterize a life lived according to the plan God has
mapped for all of humanity with gracious clarity. Paul charts this

course using the same imperative form that often gets translated with a "thou shalt" in the King James. "(Thou shalt) rejoice always. (Thou shalt) pray continually. (Thou shalt) give thanks." When I mentally add this familiar phrase that signals a holy commandment, I am reminded of the gravity implicit in Paul's writing. He's not inviting, but compelling, readers to find joy, to offer prayers, and to honor God with gratitude. Then, he underscores these commands by calling them the very backbone of Jesus's ministry and God's perfect will.

A staple in our liturgical worship every Sunday, the Lord's Prayer, pleads for God's will to be done on earth as it is in heaven. When we choose joy, prayer, and thanksgiving, we participate in the answer to that holy pleading by inhabiting the will of God, which is not a mystery to be solved but a gift to be appreciated. Choosing gratitude and joy, even in the midst of suffering and grief, opens the umbrella of God's unfailing, unassailable will, sheltering our hearts no matter which road we take or which wilderness we choose for our wandering.

Amy Linnemann

DAY SEVEN

*I know the plans I have in mind for you, declares the L*ORD*; they are plans for peace, not disaster, to give you a future filled with hope.*
Jeremiah 29:11 CEB

For ten agonizing years, I learned what it was like to forget God's promise of a future filled with hope. I entered into marriage filled with excitement and the expectation of becoming a mother. But year after year, my hopes were crushed as I struggled to conceive a child.

Hannah's story of infertility and the birth of her son in 1 Samuel became my lifeline. These pages in my Bible are permanently misshapen from being soaked with the tears accompanying my desperate prayers. But unlike Hannah, this fervent prayer of mine was never answered. The grief and disappointment created a stress my marriage was unable to sustain. I found myself alone, heartbroken, and angry with God.

I felt abandoned by the One in whom I had entrusted my future. God's silence had been deafening, so I determined to be silent too. Resigning all vestiges of hope for a family, I stopped praying altogether.

Then, late one night, God's silence ended with a powerful intervention. I dreamt I was walking in a cold, dark desert—barren, just like my life—and approached an empty darkened house. The darkness was oppressive and unsettling. But as I drew closer, I was astonished to see a hand placing a brightly lit candle in the window. It was the only point of light I could see for miles around. I entered the house, looking expectantly toward the window, and what I beheld took me to my knees.

There, standing in a shimmering gold light that encompassed his whole being, was Jesus! His hand was still on the candleholder in the window—lighting my way. I couldn't see the details of his face clearly because of the brilliant gold light, but I instantly knew him. And then he spoke the most loving words I have ever heard: "I will always be here for you, Jennifer." As he finished speaking, he began to shine brighter and started to fade—gold shimmers dispersed in an ever-widening pattern until they engulfed the whole room, swirling around me. The air in the room became effervescent. Every breath I took was full of him. Finally, the room became quiet—he was gone.

I knew I had just experienced a deeply personal miracle. While I had given up on my future, God had not. My loving Savior entered into my brokenness to assure me that he sees me, he loves me and will always be with me as I walk into the future he planned for me. Not surprisingly, that future has been blessed beyond anything I could have imagined.

While those tear-stained pages in 1 Samuel remain a precious reminder of my sorrowful connection to Hannah's story, these words of Jeremiah make my heart soar with gratitude. How marvelous it is to know we truly can trust our futures to a faithful, patient, and loving God.

Jennifer Wilder Morgan

The LORD passed before [Moses], and proclaimed,

> *"The LORD, the LORD,*
> *a God merciful and gracious,*
> *slow to anger,*
> *and abounding in steadfast love and faithfulness."*
> *Exodus 34:6*

We're probably familiar with the story of the prodigal son from Luke 15. In fact, we usually assign ourselves as either the son who walked away or the son who wasn't grateful. We very well may have been one of these two characters at some point in our lives; but do you remember the very beginning? We were created in the image of God. If the father in this prodigal son story represents God, then we ought not compare ourselves to the brothers, but strive to be like the dad.

You were made in the likeness of the Father, therefore, imitate the Father.

What does this father show in this story? Overwhelming generosity! The father has given a huge portion of his net worth to his son who completely squanders it. When his son comes back with his tail between his legs, the father doesn't berate him, he doesn't chew him out, he doesn't ask for the money back. Instead, he hugs him and throws him a party—not just any party—a lavish party. This father financially doubles down on his screwed-up son.

Who does that? God does.

You were made in the image of God. Therefore, be like God. You see, generosity flows from love and love is the DNA of the Divine. You were made in that image.

And this isn't the only time where God's generosity is on display. When God called the people of Israel out of slavery in Egypt, God needed to be reintroduced to these former slaves. God led Moses up to the top of Mount Sinai to write. God starts off by saying, "The Lord, the Lord, the compassionate and gracious God, slow to anger, abounding in love and faithfulness" (Exodus 34:6 NIV).

In this formal introduction, God leads with "I am compassionate and gracious." This is in stark contrast to the years of slavery they had just endured under Pharaoh. This compassionate and gracious God goes on to show these people lavish generosity from manna falling from the sky, to leading them into "a land flowing with milk and honey." God is making a point. God's nature is compassionate, gracious, and generous. Therefore, we were created to be compassionate, gracious, and generous too. It's in our nature.

There are two mindsets when it comes to resources: abundance or scarcity. It's hard to be compassionate, gracious, and generous if your mindset is one of scarcity. But most often humans respond to situations out of scarcity. Scarcity drives our market and our economic decisions. The scarcer a resource is, the more valuable it becomes and the less likely we are to give that resource away. Scarcity leads to selfishness, and we see selfishness all around us.

Humans live with a mindset of scarcity, yet God operates with a mindset of abundance. We are made in the image of God. Therefore, may we participate in this abundant life, one overflowing with generosity.

David Dorn II

DAY TWO

"Do not store up for yourselves treasures on earth, where moths and vermin destroy, and where thieves break in and steal. But store up for yourselves treasures in heaven, where moths and vermin do not destroy, and where thieves do not break in and steal. For where your treasure is, there your heart will be also."

Matthew 6:19-21 NIV

Author and motivational speaker Simon Sinek is credited with saying that time is our most precious commodity. I've also heard it said that being a friend is mostly about showing up. But showing up is often more difficult than it sounds. Showing up means giving up our time. It means giving away life's most precious commodity.

Recently, Jim experienced a terrible loss when his mother was tragically murdered. A shockwave went through the entire community as people tried to make sense out of what had happened. Of course, tragedies, such as this one, have no complete or sufficient answers and Jim was left grieving and broken.

As news of the event circulated among Jim's friends, an amazing thing began to happen. Jim's friends began booking flights, arranging hotel rooms, and meeting up with other friends to drive to Michigan to be with Jim. Within twenty-four hours, despite other commitments and great distances to be traveled, over a dozen of Jim's friends were seated in Jim's living room. They did not bring answers to Jim's deepest questions. They did not take away Jim's loss. They did not change the outcome of this tragic event. What they did was show up and generously offer the gift of time—life's most precious commodity.

This Scripture from Matthew has always resonated with me and has become one of my favorites. In my work as a generosity consultant, I have found it is also one of the most frequently misunderstood. Some read this Scripture and believe it suggests that when we love something, we give our treasure to it. In other words, treasure follows the heart. However, this Scripture suggests the exact opposite. Here Matthew suggests that those things we give our treasure to become the things we love. In other words, heart follows treasure.

What happens when we spend our most precious commodity, time, on our friends? What happens to the relationship when we show up and give up our time to someone else? The people with whom we share our most valued resources become those we also carry in our hearts.

What are your most precious commodities? How does your spending of life's gifts convey what you love the most? Does how you spend your time (and money) reflect what you value? If not, what might you do to better align your treasure with your heart?

Kristine Miller

DAY THREE

We know love by this, that he laid down his life for us—and we ought to lay down our lives for one another. How does God's love abide in anyone who has the world's goods and sees a brother or sister in need and yet refuses help?

Little children, let us love, not in word or speech, but in truth and action.

1 John 3:16-18

When Christians consider what it means to be generous as it relates to our everyday faithfulness, the first person who undoubtedly comes to mind for many of us is Jesus Christ.

Jesus was consistently in the business of giving aid to folks in need throughout his earthly ministry. Whether it was assuring that hungry people were fed, sick people were healed, outcast persons were reinstated within their community, or sinners like you and I were redirected from what are often death-focused ways to *the* Way, the Truth, the Life—Jesus knew what it meant to give of himself to afford those around him a healthier and more holistic existence.

In no other manner did Jesus give more of himself for others than in his death. In Jesus, God sacrificed Godself so that creation across all of time and space would be redeemed, renewed, and restored by the unwavering and unstoppable love of God. Through that sacrifice, we now know that God's love will stop at nothing to welcome us in, remind us of who we are and whose we've always been.

In 1 John 3:16, we are encouraged to remember that divine and universal belonging as we interact with our siblings in need. We, like Christ, exist to live generously for and with one another, especially when we encounter someone who is suffering. And, if we're doing it right, living in such a way will usually require us to sacrifice something—whether it be our pride, our fear, our wealth, our judgment, our status, our apathy, or our indifference.

When I was roughly eleven years old, my mom took a significant pay cut to begin a job at the middle school I attended so that she, my dad (who also worked in the school system), my sister, and I would all have the same breaks for Christmas, summer, and so on. We struggled financially during that time, but my mom went above and beyond to make sure ends were always met because the trade-off meant more quality time with us. When I think about the sacrifice she made—in pay, in her career, in her peace about our financial situation—it reminds me of how we are called to live for one another, both for our biological as well as our spiritual kin.

To be a disciple of Christ is to be—as the United Methodist Communion liturgy states—a "holy and living sacrifice in union with Christ's offering for us." Christ laid down his life for those in need throughout his earthly ministry and for all of us in his death. Christ sacrificed all to ensure we would not just know God's love by words spoken, but that we would know God's love by actions embodied.

How might you embody generosity that reflects God's unwavering and unstoppable love in this season?

What is God calling you to sacrifice for the well-being of our siblings in need?

Rev. Mary Kate Myers

DAY FOUR

Thus says the LORD:
The people who survived the sword
  found grace in the wilderness;
when Israel sought for rest,
  the LORD appeared to him from far away.
I have loved you with an everlasting love;
  therefore I have continued my faithfulness to you.
Again I will build you, and you shall be built,
  O virgin Israel!
Again you shall take your tambourines,
  and go forth in the dance of the merrymakers.
                                        Jeremiah 31:2-4

I've often wondered how much would be enough. How many pairs of shoes are enough? How big of a house is enough? How much money in the bank is enough? Sometimes I think that if I had more money, I would give more of it away to help others, but never once have I heard a billionaire say, "I think I've got enough money. I'm going to stop amassing wealth and start giving it away." To be fair, I don't actually know any billionaires, but I imagine if one did say something like that, it would make headlines.

We live in a world that is constantly telling us that we need more. Advertisers tell us that if we just had another (fill in the blank), then we would be happy. Yet, deep down most of us know that money and possessions will never truly make us happy. If we're honest with ourselves, we would probably also admit that if we had more money, we would find more ways to spend it on ourselves.

In the Book of Jeremiah, the Israelites are living under the oppression of Babylonian rule. They know that the world they are living in is not the world as it should be. It is into this reality that God speaks to the Israelites through the prophet Jeremiah saying that God's love has not ended and that God remains faithful to the Israelites. God promises that the Israelites will once again make music and enjoy fruitful vineyards, but they need to trust that God will provide for them (31:3-6).

Like the Israelites, we are a people who live in a world that is not as it should be. We live in a world that is a slave to money, consumerism, and vanity; and yet I believe that God is still speaking to us and calling us to trust that God's provision is enough for us. If we wait for the day that we have "enough" money or "enough" time or "enough" skill to live the life God is calling us to live, we will spend our whole lives waiting to be who God has called us to be. Instead, if we trust that we already have enough, we can live generous lives now, enjoying the fruitful harvests that God has already prepared for us.

Take some time to consider where in your life you feel called to be more generous. If you trust God to provide, what action can you take today to be more generous to others?

Rev. Steph Dodge

DAY FIVE

It isn't that we want others to have financial ease and you financial difficulties, but it's a matter of equality. At the present moment, your surplus can fill their deficit so that in the future their surplus can fill your deficit. In this way there is equality. As it is written, The one who gathered more didn't have too much, and the one who gathered less didn't have too little.

2 Corinthians 8:13-15 CEB

Would you do me a favor?

Take a deep breath.

Okay, now let it out.

Recently, as I was sitting in the lobby at my doctor's office, I had a you-could-knock-me-over-with-a-feather revelation. This may be common knowledge to everyone else, but it was brand-new information for me, and I can't stop thinking about it. I happened to look up at the television that loops little segments about health and wellness when a spot about asthma began. Since I have a slight touch of asthma myself, I decided to pay attention. Here's what I learned: My assumption was that, during an asthma attack, the core issue is that you can't breathe, specifically that you can't inhale. The airway constricts leaving the sufferer unable to breathe in the oxygen that is required to keep them, well, alive.

An asthma attack, I thought, was about not being able to inhale.

But that's only partially true.

The real issue is that you can't exhale. During an asthma attack it takes longer to exhale than it does to inhale, meaning the real culprit isn't that you just can't get a new breath; it's that you can't let go of an old one. Further, that breath we hold becomes toxic, because it's been transformed into carbon dioxide—something that plants need, but something that will kill us.

I was floored by this realization because it's a truth that's bigger than just asthma attacks. It gets to the heart of how we live our lives in the world, and to the point Paul is making to the Corinthian church. Stinginess is the equivalent of an asthma attack. We take a deep breath that, in the beginning, is life-giving, but once we hold it in, it transforms into a way of being that is toxic and deadly. It suffocates the journey of transformation in which we are invited to participate. Generosity functions like an asthma inhaler; it helps us release the breath we have been holding. It empowers us to breathe freely and deeply, and it allows us to participate in making the world a more just and equitable place.

Let's take another deep breath, shall we?

As you do, think about all that you've been given—maybe it's better to say that with which you have been entrusted.

Okay, now, let it out.

As you do, imagine how you can leverage all that you've been entrusted with to make the world a little more beautiful.

May it be so.

Josh Scott

DAY SIX

Jesus said to him, "If you wish to be perfect, go, sell your possessions, and give the money to the poor, and you will have treasure in heaven; then come, follow me."

Matthew 19:21

We who are privileged with riches can find it to be a curse or a blessing when trying to get into heaven. Remember, being rich is subjective for the Christian believer, especially if you live in Cité Soleil, the poorest town on the island of Haiti, which is one of the poorest countries on earth. Where I live, I'm rich by comparison. Jesus's teaching is succinct—when riches and possessions become our first love, they also become our god. Our first love should be reserved as the love we return to God by giving to those in need.

We become a blessing as disciples when we give to the poor from our heart. It means we learned to be grateful recipients of God's gifts to us from God's kingdom. What we freely received from God we freely love to give in the name of God. Even as an act of God.

In the mixture of the story about the rich ruler in the Synoptic Gospels, Matthew goes to the heart of the matter. Matthew adds a commandment in verse 19 absent in the other Gospels, and it's powerful. Jesus says, "Also, You shall love your neighbor as yourself." To grow as disciples, be grateful for your wealth that God has given you. Unload your temples of hoarded goods (storage facilities, garages, attics, pods), sell the clutter, and give the money to the poor.

"Do not be afraid, little flock, for it is your Father's good pleasure to give you the kingdom. Sell your possessions, and give alms. Make purses for yourselves that do not wear out, an unfailing treasure in heaven, where no thief comes near and no moth destroys. For where your treasure is, there your heart will be also."

Luke 12:32-34

When you feel gratitude, you're thankful for what someone did for you and also pleased by the results. Gratitude is not like indebtedness, which you are not anxious to pay back. But you are grateful and want to pay it forward. Disciples live this way.

Have you noticed how the storage facilities have become the new cathedrals for all our excess idols? Stuff we love more than our neighbors becomes stuff we love more than God. My wife and daughter discovered the experience of selling stored items and giving the funds to the poor as a mission in life. They have taken Jesus's teaching seriously by taking mounds of items in storage and going eBay crazy, selling all of the stuff they needed to let go of and sharing the earnings with those in greatest need. That's triumphant, when you gain treasures stored up in heaven!

George P. Lanier

Day Seven

This is why I thought it was necessary to encourage the brothers to go to you ahead of time and arrange in advance the generous gift you have already promised. I want it to be a real gift from you. I don't want you to feel like you are being forced to give anything. What I mean is this: the one who sows a small number of seeds will also reap a small crop, and the one who sows a generous amount of seeds will also reap a generous crop.

Everyone should give whatever they have decided in their heart. They shouldn't give with hesitation or because of pressure. God loves a cheerful giver. God has the power to provide you with more than enough of every kind of grace. That way, you will have everything you need always and in everything to provide more than enough for every kind of good work. As it is written, He scattered everywhere; he gave to the needy; his righteousness remains forever.

2 Corinthians 9:5-9 CEB

For as long as I can remember, I have heard people in churches talk about how much God loves a cheerful giver and I have long prayed that I would become one and continue in that practice. We all love a cheerful giver when you stop to think about it. Cheerful givers do so with a sense of gladness that comes from a deep well of gratitude. My friend once said that "gratitude is the superfood of the spiritual life." That thought rings true in my experience.

Second Corinthians 9 speaks of giving generously as Paul is talking about the fund-raising efforts to support Christians who are impoverished in Jerusalem. Those to whom Paul wrote were encouraged to give generously in whatever amount they could.

Paul is not so much concerned about the size of the gift as he is concerned that it comes from the heart. Yes, he notes that if you sow a small amount of seeds, you will reap a small crop and if you sow a larger amount, you will reap a larger crop. Paul is not trying to be coercive here—he states later that no one should give out of pressure. Instead, I think Paul is stating a plain truth when he speaks about the size of the crop—you will likely get out of it what you put into it, so put your heart in it. Paul then reminds them that, "God loves a cheerful giver." God loves a generous and cheerful giver who gives from the well of gratitude and joy that is tapped into when we connect with the heart of God.

Paul goes on to quote from Psalm 112 when he says, "He scattered everywhere; he gave to the needy; his righteousness remains forever." This passage is why God loves a cheerful giver. God loves a cheerful giver because God is a cheerful giver. God is like a parent delighting over a child. Parents or other adults who care for children, delight when we see things in them that remind us of ourselves because we know the feeling and are joyful about the shared experience. When Paul says that God loves a cheerful giver, it is not to shake a finger and say that if you want God to love you, you will give cheerfully. No, what Paul is saying is that when you cheerfully give, God is recognizing God's character and nature reflected in your life.

When we pray, we pray to be more like God—more Christlike. Part of our prayers are prayers of gladness that come from the well of gratitude that shapes our spiritual lives. This gratitude helps us to be more centered, more healthy, more cheerful, and more generous. I hope that you will join me in praying to become a people transformed by gladness for the life of the world.

Justin Coleman

[God said,] "So come, I will send you to Pharaoh to bring my people, the Israelites, out of Egypt." But Moses said to God, "Who am I that I should go to Pharaoh, and bring the Israelites out of Egypt?" [God] said, "I will be with you; and this shall be the sign for you that it is I who sent you: when you have brought the people out of Egypt, you shall worship God on this mountain."

But Moses said to God, "If I come to the Israelites and say to them, 'The God of your ancestors has sent me to you,' and they ask me, 'What is [God's] name?' what shall I say to them?" God said to Moses, "I am who I am."

Exodus 3:10-14a

This Scripture includes a very familiar narrative: in Exodus, after Moses goes into the wilderness and encounters the burning bush, he prays and God responds. After God gives Moses the directive to save the Israelites from slavery and lead them out of Egypt, Moses—rightfully so—questions God. Moses asks, "Who am I?" In other words, Moses questions God's direction because God's instructions seem so far out of the scope of Moses's skill set and social standing. In response, God replies with an assurance that Moses will not be alone in this endeavor.

Note that God's response is not, "You can do it!" or some sort of gifting of a new skill. God will be present with Moses because Moses is fit for the task ahead just as he is.

It is so important to note that God and Moses's interaction is prayerful. In addition, this prayer interaction is not transactional—it is a dialogue. Moses is given a task that seems impossible, and he questions God. Then God responds with an unexpected answer—not a simplistic solution to the issue but a reassurance that the road ahead is possible because God is already there.

How often do we treat prayer as a transaction? We give God our request and expect a clear-cut, simplistic answer. When churches are exploring new pathways to increased giving, we can fall into the trap of simply asking for additional funding from congregation members, making a holy opportunity for stewardship a transaction. But what would happen if we turned our hopes for additional resources into prayers to God—and we entered those prayer sessions with an expectation for dialogue rather than transaction?

This season, consider how God may be prepared to respond to your prayer dialogue with unexpected pathways to abundance. Moses was asked to do the impossible, and it worked because he was honest with God; he entered his prayer time as a dialogue, and he was reminded that God was with him, and he was not alone. In your setting, offer your requests to God as a form of holy dialogue, and be open to the unexpected opportunities God may lay in front of you.

April Casperson

DAY TWO

[Hannah said,] "Do not regard your servant as a worthless woman, for I have been speaking out of my great anxiety and vexation all this time." Then Eli answered, "Go in peace; the God of Israel grant the petition you have made to him."

1 Samuel 1:16-17

Some of us may feel like we live in a culture that intertwines our worth with our productivity. Surprisingly, Hannah may have felt the same way. In her culture, a woman's worth was closely tied to the number of children she was able to "produce," especially male children. In her day, women were always the ones held responsible for infertility, and being childless could be a reason for divorce. But her husband, Elkanah, loved her so much that instead of divorcing her, he got married to his second wife, Peninnah, with whom to have his children. In this way, Elkanah was able to escape the pressure from his own parents to have children so that he could carry on his business and family name. But the hurt ran very deep in the family, and Peninnah's insecurity provoked and irritated Hannah. It became so severe that the text reads, "it went on year by year." We can imagine why Peninnah felt bitter toward Hannah, as we see Elkanah gave Hannah the double portion of the sacrificed meat instead of their eldest son during the temple Fall Festival, according to Israelite custom. But Hannah inevitably saw that more went to Peninnah and her children even with her double portion, painfully reminding her of how "unproductive" she was in her community. So the text reports that she wept and would not eat, her heart was sad, and she was in misery.

Hannah was surrounded by all these external messages and pressures of the society that tell her, "You are worthless, and you are not enough." In fact, even her priest, Eli, thought she was drunk and worthless when she was desperately crying out to God in prayer.

But Hannah refused to internalize these external pressures provoking her, by saying "do not regard your servant as a worthless woman." Her courage to confront even her respected leader, Eli, perhaps came from her prayer earlier. Through her prayer, she aligned herself with God to view herself as "[God's] servant" and she dauntlessly fought the message that she was "worthless." Through her prayer, Hannah courageously accepted her identity as God's servant, and resisted wrapping her self-worth and identity with what the others had to say about her.

This is the power of the gift of prayer. Prayer gives us opportunities to align ourselves to God so that we may resist all the other messages that tell us we are "worthless." Through prayer, we reclaim our unconditional and sacred worthiness in God who made us in God's image to reflect God's grace and love for all. Through prayer, we gain wisdom to differentiate between "being deeply troubled" and "being worthless." We gain courage to continue being faithful in our daily lives with God's peace that surpasses all understanding.

Are you tapping into this power of prayer in your journey with God? Hannah's dauntless prayer teaches us that God, who empowered Hannah to accept her sacred worthiness in God, is ready to affirm and nurture us in our prayers no matter how daunting our circumstances are!

Rev. Danielle Buwon Kim

DAY THREE

Let my prayer stand before you like incense;
let my uplifted hands be like the evening offering.
Psalm 141:2 CEB

I am one of those people for whom strangers are just friends you haven't met yet. A trip to my local coffee shop or the library always ends up with chatting with an acquaintance in the community. My family is always waiting for me to finish talking to friends at church after worship on Sundays. These quick "hellos" and "how are you these days?" always make me smile.

However, it is important to create and maintain deep friendships as well. A close friend is someone you can call when you're having a rough day or to share joyful news. My girlfriends and I try to do "fire nights" every few weeks. We gather in our backyards and kindle a fire, putting on log after log, as we pour out what has been gathering on our hearts over the weeks.

Our relationship with God is similar to the friendships we cultivate and maintain.

As a busy mom with three small kids, I find that most of my prayer is "on the go." I lift up a prayer with my kids as we move through the drop-off line at school. I send a prayer up when I see a request from a family member come through in a text message. I try to slow down my children's hurried prayer before their song at bedtime.

But when I read the verse of Psalm 141:2, it struck a chord in my heart. These words hit the part of my soul that longs for quiet, uninterrupted time with the Lord. The time when you pour your heart out to God, and then bit by bit, your well is filled by the Spirit in return. This text reminded me that while God will hear all our hurried prayers, there is real benefit to be found in intentional time for prayer.

"Let my prayer stand before you like incense" brought forth the image of a candle burning. Lighting a special candle for your prayer time can help set intentionality. This time is set apart. You can imagine your prayers rising with the smoke of the candle, much as the psalmist writes about the incense.

The psalmist writes about "my uplifted hands." I have found that taking on the physical position of holding my hands palms up immediately opens my heart to God. I no longer feel closed off, but vulnerable in the physical posture of surrender. It is a physical way of connecting to the belief that God knows each of us intimately, there is no hiding from God.

When I get together for a fire night with my girlfriends, it requires a sacrifice of something else on my part: I miss out on dinner or bedtime with my kids. But it is worth it. Scheduling time apart to be in prayer with God is the same thing. It will require a sacrifice of your time that you might want to devote to something else. You will be tempted to continually pray with God on the go. But time spent in prayer, deepening your relationship with God, is never wasted.

Amy Sigmon

DAY FOUR

Rejoice in the Lord always; again I will say, Rejoice. Let your gentleness be known to everyone. The Lord is near. Do not worry about anything, but in everything by prayer and supplication with thanksgiving let your requests be made known to God. And the peace of God, which surpasses all understanding, will guard your hearts and your minds in Christ Jesus.

Philippians 4:4-7

When I was in my late twenties, after a few years of teaching at the high school level, I decided to go to graduate school so that I could teach at the college level. I had saved what I thought was sufficient funding to get me through the program. However, in my second year, and after a few financial setbacks (who plans for major car repairs and enormous jumps in housing and gas prices?), I found myself, even with the aid of part-time jobs, running woefully low on funds and extra high on anxiety. Every day was spent worrying about and planning how best to cobble together enough work to pay for tuition. It was apparent that if something didn't happen soon, I would have to drop out of the program and go back to work full-time.

One day, in the height of my worry and anxiety, and at the end of my rope, I stepped into the chapel on campus, sat in a pew facing the beautiful stained-glass windows and began to cry and pray: "God, I can't do this anymore. I don't know what to do next or which way to turn. I thank you that I've had the opportunity to study, to learn, and to grow. I want more than anything to stay in this program, but I can't think of a way to make it work, so I'm laying all of this at your feet. I pray that you would guide me as to what to do next." And then, something incredible happened. Immediately, a complete sense of peace washed over me, a peace that, as Paul says, "surpasses all understanding." Even though my circumstances hadn't changed, all of the anxiety and worry was completely lifted, and I knew that whatever happened, life would be okay. I left the chapel that day full of peace and joy.

I learned by accident what Paul was intentional in prescribing to his beleaguered and anxious friends in Philippi. If we want true peace and joy in our lives, we are to take everything to God in prayer. All of the things that keep us up at night, all of our worries, our joys, our desires. Everything. We ask God for what we want and for what we need. And here's the linchpin to all of it: that prayer is to be shot through "with thanksgiving." The most important ingredient in the prescription for reduced anxiety and greater joy and peace is gratitude. It's as simple as that. Offer gratitude for what is going well in your life right now, for the blessings God has bestowed on you in the past, for any small act of kindness directed your way, for the assurance that God hears your prayer, loves you, and is with you as you travel through whatever problems you may have in the moment. Offering gratitude is a means of "rejoicing" in the Lord.

When we follow Paul's recipe, we may just find that the peace of God, which surpasses all understanding, fills our hearts and minds—and that leads to joy. We cannot have peace and joy in our lives without gratitude.

In the years since I stumbled across this recipe, I have found it works every time I use it. I hope you do as well.

Rev. Susan Robb

DAY FIVE

The LORD God formed the human from the topsoil of the fertile land and blew life's breath into his nostrils. The human came to life.

Genesis 2:7 CEB

The apostle Paul advises the Thessalonian church to "pray without ceasing" (1 Thessalonians 5:17). But how could that be? We are incapable of praying continuously...unless it is as natural to us as breathing.

Perhaps it is.

Rev. Kiok Cho, a United Methodist deacon, talks about prayer from the perspective of the original garden. God forms a human creature from the earth and breathes into that one, beginning the process of respiration. Rev. Cho notes, "The first thing God did after making us from the dirt was to kiss us."

The journey from there has been a cycle of endless desire. Our desire for God and, perhaps surprisingly, God's desire for us. "Prayer is not so we can tell God many things," Rev. Cho says. "It is so that we can hear God speak God's desire for us."

When I pause to listen to my breath, to feel the movement of air through my rising and falling chest, I am drawn into that unceasing interchange. The wisdom of the ancient breath prayers, like the Jesus prayer (Inhale: "Lord Jesus Christ, Son of God"; exhale: "have mercy on me, a sinner."), is that we can participate in the prayer going on all around us when we center on our breath.

Focusing the prayer in your heart and mind allows you to completely immerse yourself in it like the air that pervades the space you inhabit. Treat it like you enter communion with God with each breath you take. You are united with the essential source of your being. Your mind is not a thing you need to tend and defend. It is something you renew with every encounter with the living God.

Focus your mind. Breathe it in like Spirit. Be re-created with every respiration. *Re-spirit-ation.* This is the ground of prayer—this reliance on breath. This awareness of presence. This drawing in and breathing out. This dance of air. In-spiring intercourse. This being in and welcoming in of the Other. The interchange of a kiss—shared breath. Peace exchanged, imparted, declared with the giving of such breath by the One who breathed life into the first of us and peace onto the disciples. I breathe in my mind, and I am in prayer.

Alex Joyner

DAY SIX

Do not be anxious about anything, but in every situation, by prayer and petition, with thanksgiving, present your requests to God. And the peace of God, which transcends all understanding, will guard your hearts and your minds in Christ Jesus.

Philippians 4:6-7 NIV

The writer of Philippians encourages us with these words. According to *Strong's Concordance*, the Greek definition of *anxious* is "to be divided, distracted." If I insert this into Philippians 4:6, it will read, "Do not be divided or distracted by anything, but in every situation, by prayer and petition, with thanksgiving, present your requests to God." To be divided means that I have two opposing forces pulling me into two different directions. Many life circumstances divide and distract us. For example, news reports can cause us to be divided, social media can cause us to be divided, and political opinions can cause us to be divided.

Our world is certainly not short of divisions and distractions. Life circumstances do their best to divide and distract us, and if we are not undergirded with, bathed in, and led by prayer, the distractions and divisions will prevail. The writer of Philippians gives us an antidote for times when we are divided and distracted: prayer. It's in prayer we petition God for what we need. Prayer is necessary and not an option. It's not something we can do today and neglect tomorrow. Prayer helps us not to live a divided and distracted life. Prayer gives us the patience we need to stand during adversity. Prayer helps us to be content in whatever circumstances we find ourselves. Prayer is the only way to not overwhelm ourselves with what is going on around us. In prayer, we find peace when we are divided or distracted. Prayer is the passageway to peace. The Scriptures say, "and the peace of God, which transcends all understanding, will guard your hearts and your minds in Christ Jesus." No other peace can do this, only the peace of God. God's peace is a gatekeeper to our hearts and minds.

I challenge you to take an inventory of your life and see where you are divided and distracted. Submit those things to God in prayer and exchange them for God's peace.

Rev. Twanda Prioleau

DAY SEVEN

Jesus took him by the hand and lifted him up, and he was able to stand. When he had entered the house, his disciples asked him privately, "Why could we not cast it out?" He said to them, "This kind can come out only through prayer."

Mark 9:27-29

A desperate father brings his son, who seems to have been possessed permanently by an unclean spirit, to Jesus to be healed. He's heard of how Jesus and his disciples have cast out numerous unclean spirits. After witnessing the disciples try and fail and argue with one another, you can imagine him being at his wit's end. Like any father who loves his child, he would do anything for his child to be healed. Which is why we hear a sense of desperation in his voice, "If you can do anything, help us! Show us compassion!"

After Jesus reminds this heartbroken dad of the power of faith, this dad cries out, "I believe; help my unbelief." This raw, vulnerable cry from a dad who is longing for his son to be healed can teach us so much about prayer. After Jesus heals this boy, the disciples wonder why they couldn't cast out the unclean spirit. Jesus replies, "This kind can come out only through prayer." Did the disciples not pray? I don't think that's the case. I think Jesus is helping us reframe our understanding of prayer. Prior to our story, the disciples were caught up in things that the world says we should care about. They were arguing over who has authority. They were arguing over who was the greatest. They were arguing over who could fill Jesus's shoes. This dad, in his prayer, was humble, acknowledging his complex faith of belief and unbelief. This dad knew Jesus could set things right. This dad knew that in Christ all things are possible.

I can't help but think that often churches and leaders end up like the disciples—caught up in what the world defines as successful. Especially now, in a world of COVID, I find myself fretting over attendance in Sunday worship, anxiously listening to finance reports, nervously trying to figure out how to bring in more dollars, more people, more volunteers, more attendees because that is what we've been taught means success. How often do we care about the standing we have, the clout we carry, or the power we wield? And yet, all Jesus wants is for us to be honest like this dad: I believe; and there are times where I wonder - help me Lord.

What would church look like if we admitted that in this season, we don't know where we are going? What would church look like if we stopped trying to have all the answers and simply prayed a vulnerable prayer like this dad? "We believe; Lord, help our unbelief." What would church look like if we remembered that prayer isn't about how elegant our words are, how long we speak, or how well we speak, but about our humble dependence upon God? What would church look like if we accepted mystery and allowed ourselves to be surprised by the amazing ways God shows up in beauty and wonder? "We believe, Lord; help our unbelief." Maybe, just maybe, if we took a page out of this dad's book and offered ourselves in raw vulnerability to the One who loves beyond measure, we might be able to see the power of reconciliation, the power of generosity, the power of relationships, the power of love. We might be able to see that to be good stewards is to abide in God's love and then to share that healing, holy love with all we meet. "We believe; Lord, help our unbelief." And in our belief and unbelief, let us remember God's love that claims us, calls us, and sends us in a love, by a love, and for a love that brings the dead to life.

Rev. Zach Moffatt

He has shown you, O mortal, what is good.
And what does the LORD require of you?
To act justly and to love mercy
and to walk humbly with your God.
                                   Micah 6:8 NIV

I'm a practical person. I like clear steps laid out, tangible things I can do to improve or work toward a goal. I think that's one of the reasons I was such a good student: I deeply appreciated a syllabus that outlined the work I was expected to do.

Perhaps that's why I'm drawn to verses like Micah 6:8. Here the prophet outlines clear steps for what God requires: do justice, embrace faithful love, and walk humbly with God. Check, check, and check.

If only it were that easy. See, I love breaking down the steps of a project and mapping out when to do what in which order to meet a deadline. But the number of projects and papers I completed in school the night before they were due is actually rather embarrassing. For all my best-laid plans, follow-through was not my strong suit. I routinely spent more time planning my schedule than actually working on the project itself.

Faithful stewardship can go awry in the same way pretty quickly. When God calls us to give faithfully, to be stewards of this earth and its resources, there is definitely an end goal in mind. But if we focus solely on the end goal, we can get caught up in the planning, the preparing, the intention, and fail to act. The purpose of stewardship has an end goal, but it also has an intermediate purpose: to shape our lives as disciples of Jesus. The practice of following God's call at each step is just as important as the end goal to which we are striving because that routine practice is what shapes us along the way. Had I followed my carefully mapped-out plans for working on papers and projects in school, I have no doubt that I would have grown much more during the process, as the final paper was simply a result of the process, not solely an end goal. This was a lesson I didn't fully learn until I became a teacher myself and started shaping projects and learning experiences for my students. It was the daily practice I wanted to instill in them, that daily practice that would shape them into learners and thinkers.

The same is true for us as faithful followers. The end goal of giving to the church is all well and good, but it's the practice of giving that shapes us as disciples. As we consider what God requires of us, we absolutely are working toward goals of justice, love, and humility; but those are not only end goals we can see far off in the future, rather they are ideals that instruct our daily actions and form us into the people God is calling us to be. May we focus on the intermediate growth offered to us along the path to faithful stewardship.

Rachel B. Hagewood

DAY TWO

With great power the apostles continued to testify to the resurrection of the Lord Jesus. And God's grace was so powerfully at work in them all.

Acts 4:33 NIV

In our mid-twenties my wife and I decided to start regularly attending church again. We both grew up going to church every week but fell out of the habit during college and in our early careers. We visited a local neighborhood Methodist church and were welcomed at the door by Sharon. Ruth made a point to greet us during the passing of the peace. Tim led beautiful music with his guitar and the choir. John frequently made BBQ for potluck. It seemed every person in the church had some amazing gift to offer. After a few Sundays, my wife and I joined the church.

One Saturday, the church decided to organize a workday. A church member put together a list of needed projects around the building. I decided to help with painting the fellowship hall. It seemed a simple task, but as I put paint on the walls, my soul awakened. I realized I was doing more than simply volunteering to do a good deed. I was responding to the call of the church. The church was inviting me to actively use my gifts in God's ongoing ministry in the world.

The disciples witnessed the ministry and miracles of Jesus firsthand. Peter and Andrew answered Jesus's call to follow. The disciples saw Jesus calm the seas in the middle of a storm. Martha saw Jesus raise Lazarus from the dead. The disciples heard Jesus teach about God's love, even as the religious leaders created traps to arrest him. Mary was the first person to encounter the risen Christ.

Forty days after Easter Sunday, the disciples were eager to know what the resurrected Jesus would do next in ministry for them. Christ did not give detailed plans for himself, but instead promised to send the power of the Holy Spirit. Then, Jesus ascended to heaven and the disciples waited.

On Pentecost Sunday, God called the church into existence. As the Holy Spirit poured out, the disciples were transformed into apostles. The apostles were no longer passive followers of Jesus, but active in ministry as they responded to God's call though the Holy Spirit. From miracles at Solomon's Colonnade to powerful proclamations of God's promise fulfilled in Christ, "With great power the apostles continued to testify to the resurrection of the Lord Jesus" (Acts 4:33a NIV).

The resurrection call to apostleship continues today. God calls us to more than weekly church attendance. God calls us to more than a successful four-week stewardship campaign. God calls us to more than simply following Jesus. God gives us the church. God gives us faithful friends. God gives every person gifts and talents. God gives us an invitation to meet the needs of our neighbors around us. In our response to God's call, we are incorporated into Christ's ongoing ministry with the promise that "God's grace was so powerfully at work in them all" (Acts 4:33b NIV).

Rev. Todd Salmi

DAY THREE

Brothers and sisters who are partners in the heavenly calling, think about Jesus, the apostle and high priest of our confession. Jesus was faithful to the one who appointed him just like Moses was faithful in God's house. But he deserves greater glory than Moses in the same way that the builder of the house deserves more honor than the house itself. Every house is built by someone, but God is the builder of everything.

Hebrews 3:1-4 CEB

It's a bold claim! An audacious metaphor! The readers of this epistle are described as active participants in the long, biblical drama of God's call and human response. We are called to be active partners in a construction project that goes all the way back to Moses, the design for which was laid out by Jesus, the Master Builder. We are partners in work on earth that will be completed in heaven! We are holy, not because of our goodness, but because we are consecrated, set apart to be used by God to share in God's saving purpose in this world.

Two congregations I pastored were engaged in major building projects. When we broke ground for the first building for a newly formed congregation in the suburbs, we knew how we positioned that building on the property would set the direction for a long-term master plan that would be completed in the future. By contrast, when we began work on the facilities of a century-old congregation in the heart of the city, we were remodeling buildings we inherited from previous generations to make them more effective tools in fulfilling a mission that began a century before we arrived.

In both congregations, we dared to believe that we were called to active, tangible, hands-on, financially generous participation in work that would outlive and outlast our efforts. We were partners in a holy calling with those who had come before us and those who would continue the work long after our phase was completed.

The construction metaphor is about much more than buildings. It is a powerful invitation to partner with God in tangible, present-day expressions of the larger vision of God's kingdom becoming a reality on earth as it will one day be completed in heaven. Holy partners in a heavenly calling are never satisfied with this world as it is, with its violence, bigotry, racism, poverty, injustice, and death. We are called to partner with God and other disciples in rebuilding this world into the world God intends for it to become.

Our calling is heavenly because our vision of the completion of the project in heaven determines the way we live right now. The goal of the holy life is not to escape this world but to partner in answering the prayer for God's kingdom to come and God's will to be done on earth as it is in heaven.

But watch out! In equally bold terms, the epistle names the urgency of our task. We are reminded of those who, because of their stubborn hearts, failed to fulfill their calling. Instead, we are called to "encourage each other every day, as long as it's called 'today'" (Hebrews 3:13 CEB).

This could be our "today." It's our opportunity to be generous partners with God, the Ultimate Builder, in God's saving, healing, life-giving work in our own place and time. Today, when we hear God's voice, may we participate generously as holy partners in a heavenly calling!

James A. Harnish

DAY FOUR

The women said to Naomi, "Blessed be the LORD, who has not left you this day without next-of-kin; and may his name be renowned in Israel! He shall be to you a restorer of life and a nourisher of your old age; for your daughter-in-law who loves you, who is more to you than seven sons, has borne him."

Ruth 4:14-15

Whose calling in the Bible is the most inspiring to you? Is it the calling of Peter who was called to be a fisher of humanity? Or Paul who was commissioned to preach the gospel to the Gentiles? For me, it is the calling of the neighboring women in the story of Ruth that inspires me the most.

The neighboring women make their first appearance in the very beginning of the story when Naomi comes back from Moab to Bethlehem with her Moabite daughter-in-law, Ruth. While it is apparent that the whole town was stirred because of them, the neighboring women are the only ones who acknowledge Naomi, saying, "Can this be Naomi?" (Ruth 1:19 NIV). This acknowledgment offers an opportunity for Naomi to express her lament: "Don't call me Naomi . . . call me Mara" (Ruth 1:20 NIV). Naomi's trauma is so deep that it changes her identity. But the neighboring women are there, listening to her grief and mourning.

Fast-forwarding a bit, Ruth is in the field of Boaz, picking up the labor of the poor at the time. As a Moabite immigrant in Bethlehem, Ruth is working among the Jews who are traditionally anti-Moabite. Making things worse, the field of Boaz is filled with danger and scarcity. Boaz has to order his men "not to lay a hand on [Ruth]" and ask Ruth to "stay close to [his] young women" (Ruth 2:9).

These Jewish neighboring women are accompanying and guiding Ruth as she tries to move forward in the field of Boaz. Their presence around her says, "Ruth belongs to us, and Ruth deserves to pursue her Bethlehemic dream."

We witness their presence at the conclusion of the story. When Ruth gives birth to Obed, it is not Ruth or Naomi, but the neighboring women who name the newborn boy and witness God's work on behalf of these two women. They prophetically speak into Naomi and Ruth's lives. "Look what God is doing in your life! You will be restored and renewed even in your old age!" This is in the moments when Naomi is still bitter because her trauma is still too deep to bring herself to celebrate. When Naomi is still struggling, it is the neighboring women who witness God's mighty work in her life.

I find the calling of the neighboring women beyond inspiring, because these women embraced Naomi and Ruth despite their traditional anti-Moabite sentiment. These women carefully listened to Naomi's trauma from the past, faithfully offered the presence of inclusivity to Ruth, and prophetically spoke hope into their lives. These women left their legacy not only in the lives of Naomi and Ruth, but in the entirety of Judeo-Christian history as Ruth is one of the ancestors of King David and Jesus. They did all these deeds while nameless and anonymous.

Every time I feel like my calling is too insignificant, or my ministry is not impactful enough, I think of the faithfulness of God who called these anonymous women to shape history. God lifts up our faithfulness of tending to the Ruths and Naomis around us, even when we feel like our ministry is insignificant and negligible. God does mighty things, like restoring people like Ruth and Naomi and shaping the course of history when we say yes to God's calling, no matter how nameless and insignificant it seems to us!

Rev. Danielle Buwon Kim

DAY FIVE

He was praying in a certain place, and after he had finished, one of his disciples said to him, "Lord, teach us to pray, as John taught his disciples." He said to them, "When you pray, say:

Father, hallowed be your name.
    Your kingdom come.
    Give us each day our daily bread.
    And forgive us our sins,
        for we ourselves forgive everyone indebted to us.
    And do not bring us to the time of trial."

Luke 11:1-4

Anyone who has been in a position of leadership has known what it is like to have every word, phrase, and decision critiqued. Most of the time, I can handle such critiques with grace . . . patience even. But that was not the case on the Sunday when someone criticized the words that I very specifically chose to wrap up the pastoral prayer and lead us in the corporate recitation of the Lord's Prayer.

Each week when I lead, I say a phrase similar to, "And hear us now, Holy God, as we pray the prayer that Jesus teaches us to pray . . ." Who knew that a vendetta against tense could lead to such frustration on the part of a parishioner! "But, Pastor Anna! It is past tense. Jesus *taught* us. Past tense." With that, I tried to with grace and patience explain why I intentionally chose (and continue to choose) the present tense.

My spouse works in a "secular" job. We were married when I was in the earlier days of my ordination process, and so as I was asked to articulate my call to committees and boards, he and I would have conversations about how call is too often seen as a driving force of "religious" vocations. He very much feels called to his work in public health, and that calling is evident in the way he works.

So when I share that I choose the present tense for how Jesus teaches us to pray, it is because I see what we call "the Lord's Prayer" as a way that we realign our lives to God's call for each of us, vocation notwithstanding. Really, what parts of our lives stand outside of the things Jesus models that we ask for?

- May we always speak of God with reverence and respect
- Let your will be what orders all of creation
- Give us a fair portion of sustenance
- Forgive us as much as we can forgive others
- Let us see hardship as an equal, surmountable part of life

There are times in my job where I want to shout, "If I have to handle one more task that Jesus wouldn't have cared about…" but as Jesus continues to teach me to pray, I put myself back in alignment with God's call not only for my *job* but for my whole life. It is not only the vocationally religious who ask for this alignment, but all of us. Each person who has articulated a desire to Jesus gets to articulate prayers exactly how Jesus teaches us to pray…and what a gift when, after patient explanation, that "tense" parishioner realized that the Lord's Prayer is present.

Rev. Anna C. Guillozet

DAY SIX

The Spirit said to Philip, "Go over to this chariot and join it." So Philip ran up to it and heard [an Ethiopian court official] reading the prophet Isaiah. He asked, "Do you understand what you are reading?" He replied, "How can I, unless someone guides me?" And he invited Philip to get in and sit beside him.

Acts 8:29-31

Have you ever found yourself asking, "What am I doing here?" Every time I read this text I wonder if that was what was going on in Philip's mind as the Spirit led him to a desert road. After an amazing experience in Samaria where God worked signs and wonders through him, Philip now stood on a desert road about to experience an unlikely and transformative encounter.

I love this story, primarily, because in it we see God's love in action—welcoming those who once stood well beyond the margins. Secondarily, I love this story because Philip began his encounter with a question, and I love questions. This is something I have enjoyed since early childhood. As a child, this love of questions manifested itself as a fascination for the "how" and "why" of things. A couple of times, around ages seven or eight, I became so curious about electricity and how plugging an iron into the wall created heat, that I took my mother's iron apart. On both occasions I almost set our house on fire. I find questions to be good companions in the journey of faith and life, for they create opportunities for connections and discovery.

Philip also seemed to share a certain love for questions. As he followed the direction of Spirit, we hear him ask a very important one, "Do you understand what you are reading?" Philip's question did not seek to patronize or demean this fellow traveler. Much to the contrary, it served as an opportunity to connect and grow in relationship.

Sometimes it takes a physical or spiritual displacement—like the desert road, a global pandemic, or any other situation that moves us beyond our states of comfort—to make us more sensitive to God's transformative work in the world. The Ethiopian was a high-ranking official in the royal court. He was a learned individual, who, though able to comprehend the words before him, lacked the understanding needed for transformation. This man could have ignored Philip. He could have chosen to look down on this stranger standing by the road. But, in a move of remarkable self-awareness and humility, he engaged, responding, "How can I, unless someone guides me?" Philip's question led to another question, an offer of hospitality, and a journey to transformation.

Philip's encounter with the Ethiopian offers us a reminder that each of us is called to journey with others. The love of God we find in Jesus Christ is not a secret to be kept but good news to be shared. Philip's physical displacement offered him an opportunity to engage in the great work of love active in the world. When you find yourself feeling out of place, be attentive to the whispers of the Spirit. Perhaps you will also encounter somebody in need of understanding.

Rev. Jefferson M. Furtado

DAY SEVEN

Now in Joppa there was a disciple whose name was Tabitha, which in Greek is Dorcas. She was devoted to good works and acts of charity.

Acts 9:36

Unlike the twelve disciples, we do not learn from Scripture Tabitha's call to become a disciple of Jesus. While too many women in Scripture go unnamed and unacknowledged, she is mentioned in two languages. A double honor. Some say mentioning both versions of her name alludes to her far-reaching impact on multiple, diverse communities. *Tabitha* means "gazelle" or "deer."

Tabitha is named and identified as a disciple. This demarcation is significant because she is the only woman explicitly named a disciple in the New Testament. We know there were many women who were disciples of Jesus; however, Tabitha is the only one identified as such.

One translation of *disciple* is "learner." This definition, however, is shortsighted and has created generations of learned people who do not follow, as in practice acts and express emotions of loving for Jesus. Learning and doing are not one and the same. Disciples both proclaim and practice the Greatest Commandment (Matthew 22:34-40) and the Great Commission (Matthew 28:19-20).

Too often in search of our special or specific call, we forget the foundational call as a disciple to love God, love self, love neighbor (Matthew 22). Motivated by love, Tabitha cares for widows in the community by sewing them tunics. In addition to understanding widows as those whose husbands died, we can also look at what that symbolized. It was about loss of protection, care, safety, family, and sustenance. If we consider these losses, then "widows" are all around us.

We do not know what more Tabitha did for the widows, if anything. However, I imagine that genuine connection through conversation was part of her interaction with them. She loved them so much that when she died, the community mourned.

Perhaps gratitude for and living out the disciple's call to love leads to clarity of a more specific, gifts-centered call. What if by living out the first call the other becomes more apparent in time? What if they are intricately linked together?

There is no greater call than to the call we all have to love; love that is professed, felt, and practiced.

Tabitha's love for Jesus and her impact in the Joppa community and beyond is remembered in Scripture. The story of her resurrection is one that spread throughout time. At the same time, her story remains one that is not highlighted or preached often. We may only know of her because of a sewing circle donning her name. Yet, in just a few verses we meet a loving woman disciple who loved God and her community.

Perhaps we have complicated our understanding of call by searching high and low for a way to make an impact and be purposeful. We cannot bypass our call as disciples of Jesus in search for some greater way to serve, for it is expected, even commanded, to be at the center of who we are—as it was for Jesus.

Charity Goodwin